Waltham Fore
Please return this item by the last
renewed unless required by another customer.
KT-381-747
Mar 2013 | 02 JUL 2013

LOST CITIES

NICOLA BARBER

Raintree

WALTHAM FOREST LIBRARIES
904 000 00241913

Raintree is an imprint of Capstone Global Library Limited, a company incorporated in England and Wales having its registered office at 7 Pilgrim Street, London, EC4V 6LB – Registered company number: 6695582

To contact Raintree please phone 0845 6044371, fax + 44 (0) 1865 312263, or email myorders@raintreepublishers.co.uk. Customers from outside the UK please telephone +44 1865 312262.

Text © Capstone Global Library Limited 2013
First published in hardback in 2013
The moral rights of the proprietor have been asserted.

All rights reserved. No part of this publication may be reproduced in any form or by any means (including photocopying or storing it in any medium by electronic means and whether or not transiently or incidentally to some other use of this publication) without the written permission of the copyright owner, except in accordance with the provisions of the Copyright, Designs and Patents Act 1988 or under the terms of a licence issued by the Copyright Licensing Agency, Saffron House, 6–10 Kirby Street, London EC1N 8TS (www.cla.co.uk). Applications for the copyright owner's written permission should be addressed to the publisher.

Edited by Laura Knowles, Adam Miller, Harriet Milles, and Helen Cox Cannons
Designed by Victoria Allen
Original illustrations © Capstone Global Library Ltd 2013
Illustrated by Martin Bustamante
Picture research by Tracy Cummins
Originated by Capstone Global Library Ltd.
Production by Alison Parsons
Printed and bound in China by Leo Paper Products Ltd

ISBN 978 1 406 24968 2
16 15 14 13 12
10 9 8 7 6 5 4 3 2 1

British Library Cataloguing in Publication Data
Barber, Nicola.
Lost cities. -- (Treasure hunters)
930.1-dc23
A full catalogue record for this book is available from the British Library.

Acknowledgements
We would like to thank the following for permission to reproduce photographs:
Alamy pp.4 (©Robert Harding Picture Library Ltd), 33 bot (©Imagestate Media Partners Limited - Impact Photos); Art Resource pp.16 (Gianni Dagli Orti/The Art Archive, 34 (Dietrich Gra/Ethnologisches Museum, Staatliche Museen, Berlin, Germany); Corbis pp.5 (©Ira Block/National Geographic Society), 14 top (©George Steinmetz), 15 (©K.M. Westermann), 17 (©Bettmann), 21 (©Hulton-Deutsch Collection), 28 bot (©Mimmo Jodice), 29 & 31 (©Roger Ressmeyer), 36 (©Arne Hodalic); Getty Images pp.13 (©John Mitchell), 22 (©Time & Life Pictures), 25 (©Alberto Incrocc); NASA p. 12 top; National Geographic p.39 (©BINGHAM, HIRAM - YALE PEABODY MUSEUM); Newscom pp.9 (©Donald Nausbaum/Robert Harding), 18 (akg-images/Peter Connolly), 20, 23, 35 (©akg-images), 37 bot (©AFP PHOTO/AFP/Getty Images); Photoshot p.10 (©UPPA); Reuters p.41(©Pilar Olivares); Shutterstock pp.1 (©Pani), 6 (©Lukasz Kurbiel), 7 (©Connors Bros.), 8-9 (©apdesign), 11 (©Rechitan Sorin), 12 bot (©Mechanik), 14 bot (©Iwona Grodzka), 19 (©Eky Studio), 24 (©Catmando), 28 top (©Warren Goldswain), 30 (©Alfio Ferlito), 31 bot (©Joy Fera), 31 mid (©Jelena Voronova), 32 (©kated), 33 t.l. (©J. Helgason), 33 t.r. (©Scisetti Alfio), 37 top (©Galyna Andrushko), 38 (©Arvind Balaraman), 40 (©Steve Estvanik), 42 (©Patrick Poendl), 43 (©Linda Bucklin). Design features: Shutterstock.

Cover photo of Angkor Wat, Ta Prohm temple, Cambodia, Shutterstock (©davidk).

Waltham Forest Libraries

904 000 00241913

Askews & Holts	19-Feb-2013
C930.1 BAR	£8.99
3785651	

Expert consultant
We would like to thank Dr Mark Horton for his invaluable help in the preparation of this book. Dr Horton is Professor in Archaeology at the University of Bristol and a specialist in the archaeology of historical societies around the world.

CONTENTS

Looking for lost cities 4

Ubar: city in the sands 8

The search for Troy 16

Pompeii: buried alive 24

Lost cities of the Incas 34

Legends of lost cities 42

Timeline 44

Glossary 45

Find out more 46

Index 48

LOOKING FOR LOST CITIES

How do cities get lost? It's a good question! Think of one of the world's many modern-day cities, such as London, or Los Angeles, or Tokyo, and it's difficult to imagine how they could ever be "lost". Ancient cities were, of course, many times smaller than our modern-day mega-cities. And over the centuries many of them have indeed been abandoned and forgotten.

Mohenjo-Daro in modern-day Pakistan was one of the world's earliest cities. It was abandoned in around 1800 BC.

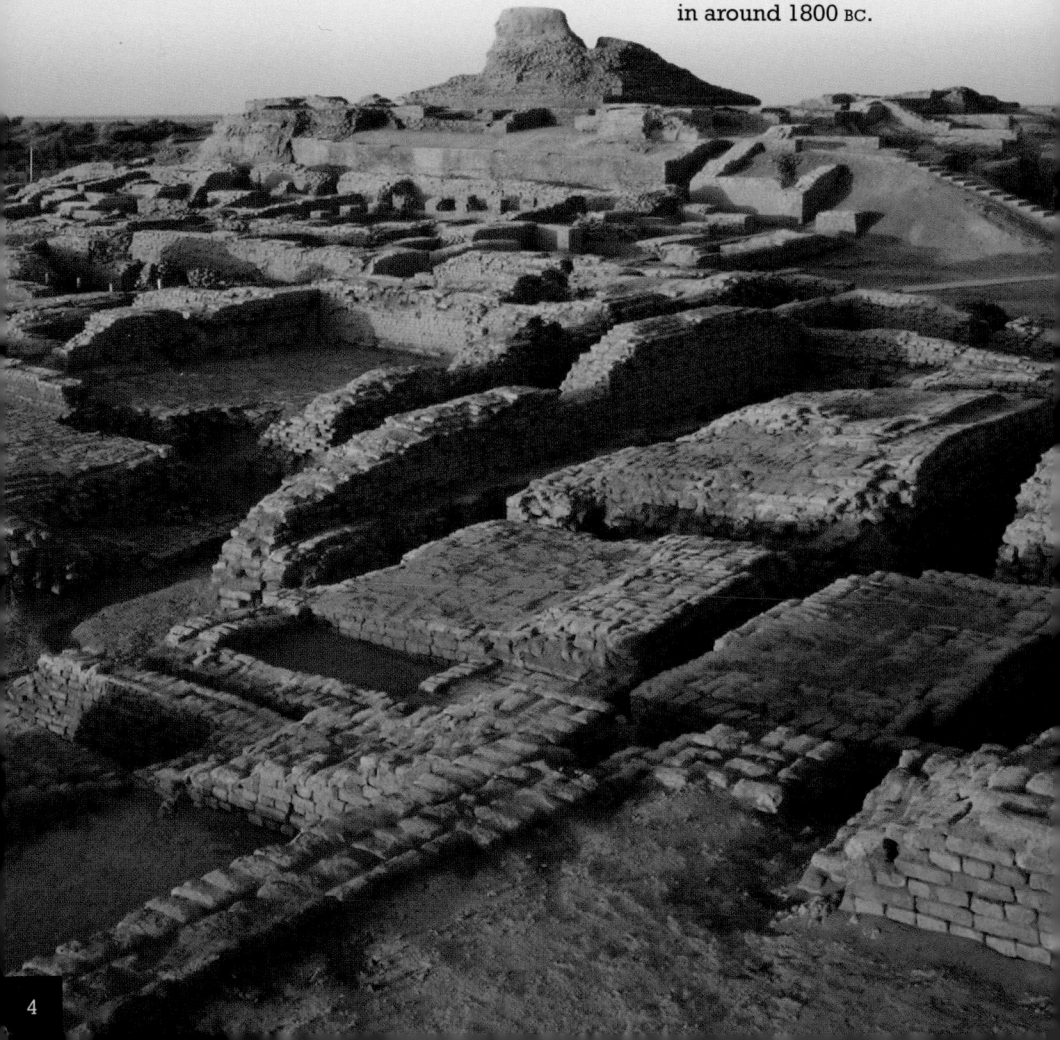

WHAT HAPPENED?

There are many reasons why a city can become lost. In some cases, a natural disaster such as an earthquake, a volcanic eruption, or flooding has simply overwhelmed a city. This is what happened to Pompeii in Italy when the volcano Vesuvius erupted violently. You can find out more about the swift and terrifying destruction of Pompeii on pages 24–33.

Other cities were abandoned by their inhabitants because of war. In some places, the food or water supply seems to have been disrupted, forcing a city's residents to move elsewhere. But sometimes we just don't know why a place that had once been bustling and busy was deserted by the people who lived there.

In AD 1250, on the floodplain of the Mississippi river (in modern-day United States), there stood one of the biggest cities in the world. At that time, the city of Cahokia covered nearly 15 square kilometres (6 square miles) and was home to up to 20,000 people – as big as London or Paris at the time. Yet by 1400 it had been abandoned. Today, the only reminders of this once-thriving city are more than 100 earth mounds (see photo below).

LOST... AND FOUND

Most "lost" cities are not absolutely lost. Local people often know something about the mysterious ruins that lie deep in a jungle, or are covered by desert sands. But it's only when an outsider comes along to investigate that people realize what these ruins really are.

This is what happened to the American historian and explorer Hiram Bingham, high in the Andes Mountains in 1911. Bingham was looking for the lost cities of the Inca people. He was amazed when a local guide led him to some spectacular ruins, high on a mountain top. Although Bingham was not the first to find the ruins, he was the first person to bring them to the attention of the wider world. You can find out more about Bingham's "discovery" on pages 34–41.

Machu Picchu in the Andes Mountains.

"IT IS PERCHED ON A MOUNTAIN TOP IN THE MOST INACCESSIBLE CORNER OF THE MOST INACCESSIBLE SECTION OF THE URUBAMBA RIVER. SO FAR AS I KNOW, THERE IS NO PART OF THE ANDES THAT HAS BEEN BETTER DEFENDED BY NATURE."

HIRAM BINGHAM DESCRIBING THE REMOTE LOCATION OF THE LOST CITY OF MACHU PICCHU IN AN ARTICLE HE WROTE FOR NATIONAL GEOGRAPHIC MAGAZINE.

The magnificent ruins of Angkor Wat temple in Cambodia are part of what was once a huge city from the 800s to the 1400s.

WHY LOOK?

Why do people look for lost cities? Historians and archaeologists want to know more about the people who once lived there: what they ate, who they worshipped, what jobs they did. And there is always the chance that something really unusual may turn up, including treasure – gold or silver!

UBAR: CITY IN THE SANDS

Sand, sand, and more sand… The Rub al-Khali (Arabic for the "Empty Quarter") is the largest area of uninterrupted sand in the world. It covers much of the southern Arabian Peninsula, with wind-blown dunes rising up to 300 metres (984 feet) high. It is fiercely hot, very dry, and virtually uninhabited.

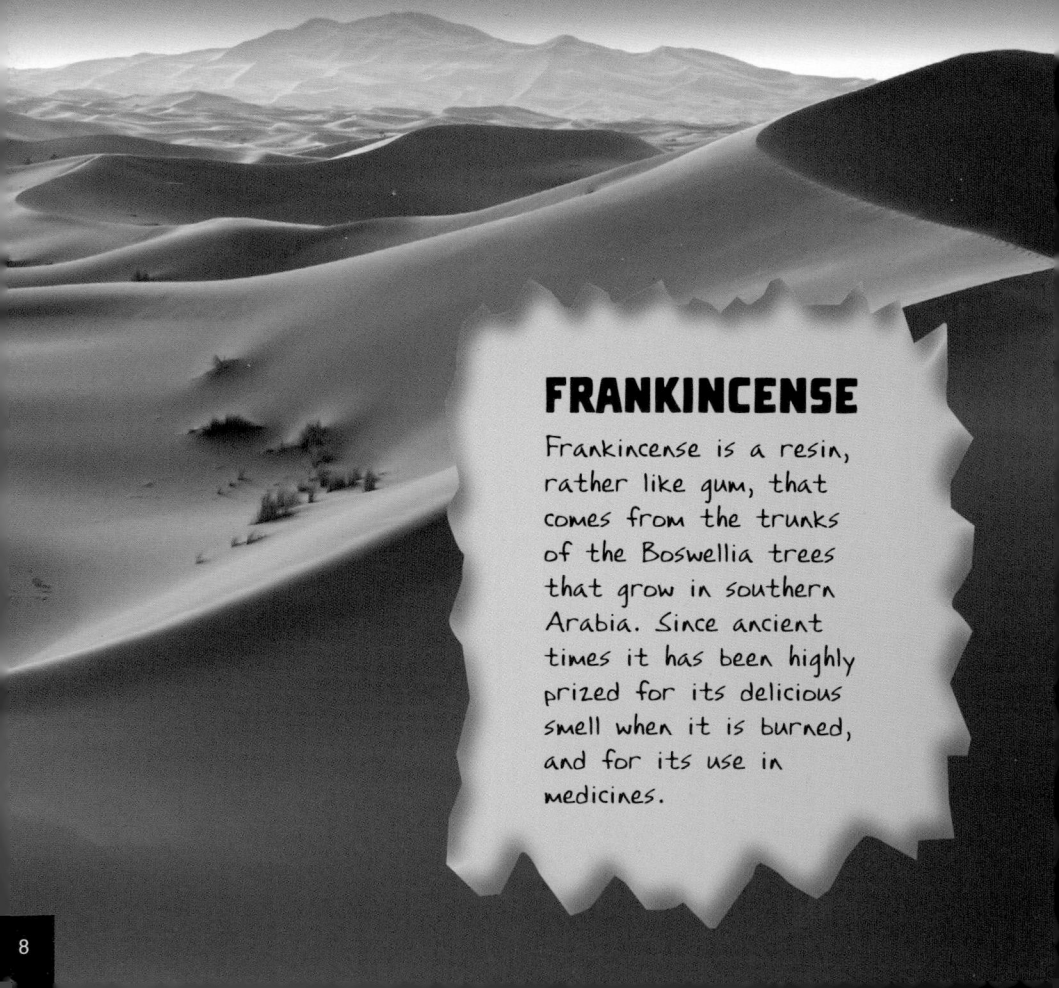

FRANKINCENSE

Frankincense is a resin, rather like gum, that comes from the trunks of the Boswellia trees that grow in southern Arabia. Since ancient times it has been highly prized for its delicious smell when it is burned, and for its use in medicines.

THE ANCIENT PEOPLE OF 'AD

Tales of a fabulous city that had long-since disappeared beneath the sands of the Rub Al-Khali have been passed down for centuries. References to such a city appear in the holy book of Islam, the Qur'an. The nomadic people of the deserts, the Bedouin, also have many stories about an ancient trading city inhabited by the people of 'Ad.

According to these tales, the city was famed for its trade in frankincense, but its people became arrogant and were punished when the city suffered a terrible calamity and was destroyed.

"NOW THE 'AD BEHAVED ARROGANTLY THROUGH THE LAND, AGAINST (ALL) TRUTH AND REASON, AND SAID: 'WHO IS SUPERIOR TO US IN STRENGTH?'"

HOW THE PEOPLE OF 'AD ARE DESCRIBED IN THE QUR'AN

DANGEROUS LANDS

The tales of the lost city in the sands fascinated explorers. But a trip into the Rub al-Khali was not to be undertaken lightly. The desert covers an area bigger than France, and has extremes of temperatures ranging from over 50°Celsius (122°Fahrenheit) during the day to below freezing at night. With few sources of water, this was not a place to get lost in.

Harry St John Philby was a fluent Arabic speaker and wore Bedouin clothes. In 1932, he crossed the Rub al-Khali of Arabia.

RACE ACROSS THE SANDS

In 1931, a British explorer called Bertram Thomas became the first European to make the journey across the Rub al-Khali. In doing so he beat his fellow-explorer and friend, Harry St John Philby, who had hoped and planned to be the first to cross the desert sands.

Once Philby had recovered from his disappointment, he resolved to go anyway. In fact, Philby wanted to do more than just cross the Rub al-Khali. He wanted to look for the city the Bedouins had told him about – a city called Ubar.

Philby started his journey across the "ocean of sand" that is the Rub al-Khali with 32 camels and 15 Bedouin men.

Spotted from space

It was modern technology that allowed archaeologists finally to locate the long-lost city of Ubar. Images taken from space can show up marks on Earth's surface that cannot be seen from the ground. In the Rub al-Khali, pictures taken by the *Challenger* Space Shuttle revealed ancient tracks created thousands of years ago by camel caravans. And it seemed that many of these tracks led to Ubar.

FOLLOWING CLUES

Philby did not find Ubar, and neither did several later expeditions. But the pictures taken from the Space Shuttle, and others from satellites, gave explorers and archaeologists some vital clues.

In the 1990s, an expedition that included American film-maker Nicholas Clapp, British explorer Ranulph Fiennes, and American archaeologist Juris Zarins set out into the Rub al-Khali.

These images of the Rub al-Khali were both taken by satellites. The site of Ubar is too small to show up, but tracks leading to the site helped archaeologists to work out where it was.

RUINS ARE FOUND!

Even with all the information from the space images, it still took a great deal of painstaking and patient work before Clapp's expedition finally found what it had been looking for. At a watering hole called Shis'r, there was an old Arab fort. But beneath and around the fort lay older ruins. Were these the remains of Ubar?

DANGER: SNAKES!

If you ever find yourself on an archaeological dig in the desert, remember to keep an eye out for snakes! Hiding under the boxes in the supply tent, the expedition found an unremarkable-looking small brown snake. It turned out to be a deadly carpet viper – very poisonous and very bad-tempered! Luckily, no one was bitten.

EXCAVATIONS

The excavations at Shis'r uncovered a small settlement with a fort, walls, and watchtowers. The people of this ancient city drew water from a well fed by water in a cave, deep underground. This water was vital for the inhabitants – it was the only water for hundreds of kilometres. Travelling camel caravans also stopped there to replenish their supplies. But excavations quickly revealed that the source of the water also brought about the city's downfall around 800 years ago.

THE SINKHOLE

The legends of Ubar told how the city had come to a terrible end when it sank into the sands of the desert. The truth behind the legend appeared to lie in the large sinkhole at Shis'r. A sinkhole is a hole in the ground formed when the roof of an underground cave collapses below. When the cave beneath the well collapsed at Shis'r, it took much of the city with it. Did this prove that the city was indeed Ubar?

In this aerial view, you can see the modern settlement at Shis'r beyond the hole that swallowed up the ancient city.

WAS THIS UBAR?

From around 3200 BC until its sudden collapse in around AD 300, the ancient settlement at Shis'r was a thriving place on the route of the frankincense trade. Camel caravans stopped at the city to fill up with water and supplies before setting off across the Rub al-Khali, loaded with valuable frankincense.

Today, experts around the world still disagree about whether this was the fabled city of Ubar or not. Many now believe that Ubar was the name of a region rather than a city. But they do agree that the excavations at Shis'r were of great importance for our understanding of life in ancient Arabia.

WHAT DID THEY FIND?

The archaeologists working at the Shis'r site didn't find any gold or treasure. But they did find pieces of pottery from far-distant lands – Persia, Rome, and Greece. These suggested that the city was indeed once a busy trading centre. The sturdy city walls and watchtowers were probably built to defend the precious supply of water from raiding Bedouin tribes.

These are what some people believe are the ruins of the city of Ubar.

The Search for Troy

Imagine starting work on an archaeological excavation to find a long-lost city, and then digging up not just one city – but nine! This is exactly what happened to the German businessman and archaeologist Heinrich Schliemann.

Ever since he was a small boy, Schliemann had been fascinated by the legendary city of Troy. At that time, no one knew whether Troy was a real place, or whether it was just a make-believe city in stories and poems. Schliemann was determined to find out.

Stories of Troy

As a child, Schliemann's favourite story came from the *Iliad*, an epic poem written by the ancient Greek poet Homer. In the *Iliad*, Homer recounts the events of a few weeks in the long-running war between the Greeks and the people of Troy – the Trojans. During this war, the city of Troy was besieged by the Greeks for 10 long years. The war finally ended with the destruction of the city.

HEINRICH SCHLIEMANN

Born: 1822

Died: 1890

- According to Schliemann, as a boy of seven years old, he vowed to find the true location of the real Troy.
- One of Schliemann's first jobs was as a cabin boy on a ship that was wrecked during a storm off the coast of Holland.
- Schliemann taught himself many languages, including English, Dutch, Russian, French, Spanish, Portuguese, and Italian.
- Schliemann made a fortune working in Russia trading indigo dye, and during the Gold Rush in California, USA.

THE SEARCH BEGINS

In 1863, Schliemann decided to retire from business. He was so wealthy that he had enough money to devote the rest of his life to his great obsession – the search for Troy. Using clues from Homer's *Iliad*, Schliemann travelled to Turkey to begin the search for likely sites.

Schliemann was not alone in his quest. Another amateur archaeologist, a British man called Frank Calvert, had done some excavations at a mound in a remote spot called Hisarlik in western Turkey. Calvert convinced Schliemann that Hisarlik could be the site of ancient Troy.

Is this what the ancient city of Troy once looked like?

WHICH CITY?

Schliemann began excavating at Hisarlik in 1871. With teams of local workers he sunk deep shafts down into the mound. It soon became apparent that there was a whole series of ancient cities buried beneath the mound, one on top of another. Clearly Troy had been destroyed and rebuilt many times. But which one was Homer's Troy?

In his determination to get down to the bottom – and oldest – layer, Schliemann ordered his workers to move huge amounts of stone and rubble. But when Schliemann examined the ruins at the bottom of the trenches, he decided they were too old to be those of Homer's Troy.

Working back up, he came across layers of ash that suggested evidence of fire. In the *Iliad*, Homer describes how Troy was burned to the ground by the Greeks. Schliemann decided that this was the layer of remains he needed to excavate. Unfortunately, the earlier digging had destroyed a large area of the city Schliemann now believed was Troy.

UNCOVERING TREASURE

In 1873, the workers at Hisarlik uncovered a town wall and a great gate. These were important finds, but Schliemann was on the lookout for something even more exciting. According to Homer, Priam was the ruler of Troy during the war with the Greeks. Schliemann firmly believed that as the siege of the city dragged on, Priam must have found somewhere to hide his most precious belongings.

In May 1873, something happened to convince him that he was right. While clearing rubble away from a wall, Schliemann caught sight of the glint of metal. He immediately sent his workmen for a lunch break so that he could examine his find secretly.

Schliemann's excavations at Troy revealed walls and a great gate.

"WHILE THE MEN WERE RESTING AND EATING, I CUT OUT THE TREASURE WITH A LARGE KNIFE. THIS ... INVOLVED GREAT RISK, SINCE THE WALL OF THE FORTIFICATION BENEATH WHICH I HAD TO DIG THREATENED EVERY MOMENT TO FALL ON ME. BUT THE SIGHT OF SO MANY OBJECTS, EVERY ONE OF WHICH IS OF INESTIMABLE VALUE TO ARCHAEOLOGY, MADE ME RECKLESS. I NEVER THOUGHT OF ANY DANGER."

SCHLIEMANN DESCRIBING HIS DISCOVERY OF "PRIAM'S TREASURE"

PRIAM'S TREASURE

The so-called "Priam's treasure" (shown here), included a copper shield, a beautiful silver vase, many gold and copper plates and cups, and fine golden jewellery. In fact, we now know that this treasure had nothing to do with Priam, but came from a layer over 1,000 years older than "Homeric" Troy.

SMUGGLING AND LIES

According to the account written by Schliemann, he removed the treasure from the ground and handed it to his wife, Sophia, who wrapped the precious objects in her scarf. Under the terms agreed for the excavation, Schliemann was supposed to share any treasure found at the site half-and-half with the Turkish authorities. To avoid this, Schliemann smuggled the treasure out of Turkey and hid it in Greece.

In 1874, Schliemann published a book about his findings at Hisarlik, and his wife Sophia appeared in public wearing the jewellery found at Troy. The Turkish authorities were furious when they realized what Schliemann had done. In the end, Schliemann traded some of the treasure with the Turkish government and paid a large fine. Only then was he allowed to go back to Hisarlik to continue the excavations.

In this photo, Schliemann's wife, Sophia, wears some of the jewellery found at the excavation of Troy.

The treasure kept by Schliemann never went back to Turkey. It ended up in the Royal Museums of Berlin, in Germany. During World War II it was carefully packed away and hidden in a bunker beneath Berlin Zoo. But in the last days of the war, Soviet troops found it, and it was stolen once again. It disappeared completely until 1993, when it was put on display in Moscow. Despite some negotiations for its return, it is still there.

TROY TODAY

The excavations that continue at Hisarlik today are rather more organized and scientific than Schliemann's! Archaeologists now believe that the mound contains the remains of ten settlements, spanning 4,500 years of occupation. Troy was built at the crossing point between Europe and Asia, which made it a target throughout its history. This explains why it was such a well-defended fortress.

POMPEII: BURIED ALIVE

IT IS THE MORNING OF 24 AUGUST, AD 79. IN THE ROMAN CITY OF POMPEII IN SOUTHERN ITALY, THERE IS A SENSE OF UNEASE IN THE AIR. THERE HAVE BEEN A FEW EARTH TREMORS OVER THE PAST FEW DAYS. FOR MANY IN THE CITY, THESE SMALL TREMORS BRING BACK MEMORIES OF A BIG EARTHQUAKE THAT DEVASTATED PARTS OF THE CITY 17 YEARS AGO, IN AD 62. IS THERE ANOTHER EARTHQUAKE ON THE WAY?

VESUVIUS

For any townspeople in Pompeii who looked towards the top of the mountain that lay close to the city, the sense of unease may have got worse. A red glow in the sky showed that this was no ordinary mountain. It was a volcano – and it was active. But Mount Vesuvius had not erupted for nearly 300 years, and no one in Pompeii had any reason to believe it was about to do so. When Vesuvius blew its top, the people of Pompeii were completely unprepared.

The ancient Romans did not know, as we do today, that earth tremors can be a sign that a volcano is about to erupt.

This is the crater of Mount Vesuvius today.

PLINY'S LETTER

We know about the eruption from an eyewitness account in a letter written by an ancient Roman lawyer, Pliny the Younger. Pliny was staying at a nearby town and was close enough to see the eruption.

"ASHES WERE ALREADY FALLING, NOT AS YET VERY THICKLY. I LOOKED ROUND: A DENSE BLACK CLOUD WAS COMING UP BEHIND US, SPREADING OVER THE EARTH LIKE A FLOOD ... WE HAD SCARCELY SAT DOWN TO REST WHEN DARKNESS FELL, NOT THE DARK OF A MOONLESS OR CLOUDY NIGHT, BUT AS IF THE LAMP HAD BEEN PUT OUT IN A CLOSED ROOM."

Pompeii's last day
1 Mount Vesuvius begins to erupt on the morning of 24th August, AD 79
3 Many townspeople flee the city. Those who stay face certain death.

4 Around midnight, a deadly pyroclastic flow of hot ash, rocks, and gas flows down the sides of the volcano at a speed of around 100 kilometres (62 miles) per hour

2 Ash and volcanic rocks fall on to the streets of Pompeii

A VIOLENT END

The eruption of Vesuvius on 24 August AD 79 lasted more than 24 hours. There was little chance to escape. Ash and pumice (solidified lava) rained down on the city, burying everything in a layer up to 3 metres (10 feet) thick. People took refuge in their houses, or ran towards the sea.

But then came violent surges of hot gas mixed with ash and rock that cascaded down the mountain at speeds of up to 100 kilometres (62 miles) per hour. These surges killed all those who had managed to survive the first few hours. Thousands of people died in and around Pompeii.

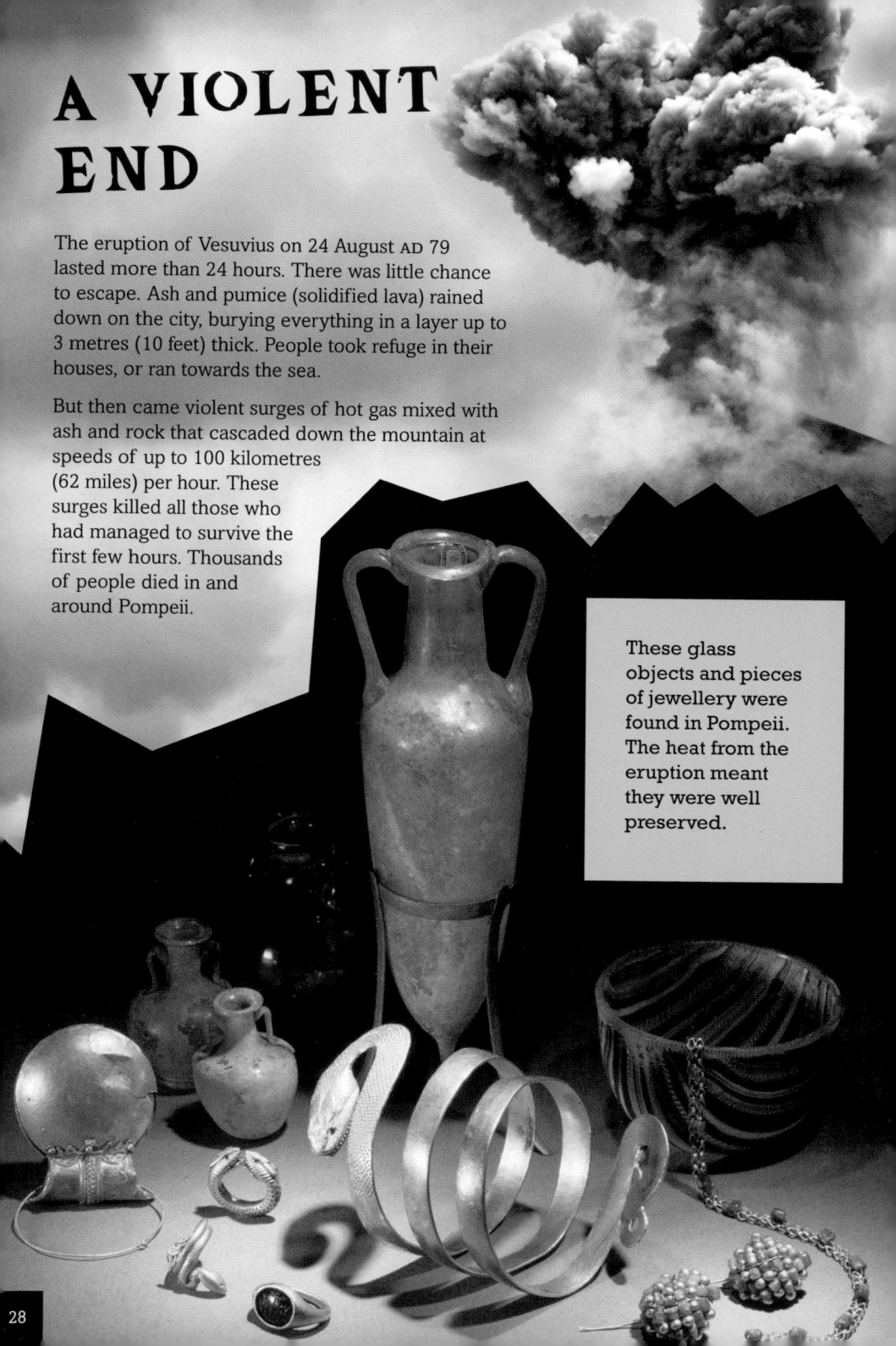

These glass objects and pieces of jewellery were found in Pompeii. The heat from the eruption meant they were well preserved.

BURIED AND FORGOTTEN

The disaster was so catastrophic that the Romans made no attempt to rebuild the city. It lay buried beneath a thick layer of ash and mud for more than a thousand years. The name of Pompeii was forgotten.

In the 1700s, workmen digging in the area uncovered some of the remains, and soon there was great interest in the buried city. When a stone bearing the inscription *Rei publicae Pompeianorum* ("commonwealth of Pompeians") was uncovered in 1763, the city even got its name back.

Today, the ruins of Pompeii are uncovered once again. You can see Mount Vesuvius in the background.

Fishy evidence

Evidence for the date when Vesuvius erupted comes from written sources such as Pliny the Younger's letters. But this evidence has recently been confirmed by a more unusual investigation. Scientists have analysed traces of fish sauce (see page 33) found in jars in Pompeii. From the type of fish used to make the sauce, and the state of the sauce, they are sure that the eruption happened around the end of August, AD 79.

PLUNDERING POMPEII

The first people to excavate Pompeii were interested only in the treasures – the wall paintings, statues, jewellery – that could be removed. They were quite happy to smash down walls, and to remove paintings and mosaics to get what they wanted.

It was an Italian archaeologist, Giuseppe Fiorelli, who finally put a stop to the plunder. When Fiorelli took over in 1860, he divided the city into nine sections and organized methodical excavations, layer by layer. He made careful notes of where things were found.

GIUSEPPE FIORELLI

Born: 1823

Died: 1896

- *He first worked at Pompeii in the 1840s, but in 1848 was imprisoned by the king of Naples because of his political (and archaeological) views.*
- *He founded a school of archaeology and pioneered many of the techniques still used in archaeology today.*
- *The technique of making plaster casts, invented by Fiorelli, is today known as the Fiorelli process.*

This is one of the mosaics found in Pompeii.

Plaster casts

Fiorelli invented a way of preserving the shapes of the bodies of the people who had died in the city. After the eruption, the volcanic ash had set hard around the victims' bodies. Over time, the bodies had decayed away to nothing, leaving hollows in the ash. Fiorelli realized that these hollows were like moulds. If he filled the moulds with plaster, he would recreate the exact shapes of the victims' bodies. The results were amazingly and uncomfortably life-like (see above)!

FROZEN IN TIME

The uncovering of Pompeii revealed an ancient Roman city, frozen in time. What makes Pompeii so special for archaeologists and ancient historians today is that this was an ordinary city, with people going about their ordinary business. We have learned huge amounts about everyday life in Roman times from the excavations at Pompeii.

WORK AND PLAY

Pompeii was a bustling and thriving city in AD 79. There were markets, shops, workshops, inns, and a flourishing woollen industry. The people of Pompeii also enjoyed their leisure time at the baths, at the theatre, and at the games.

CAVE CANEM! (BEWARE OF THE DOG!)

Visitors to one of the houses uncovered in Pompeii were greeted with this warning, spelt out in a mosaic on the floor. Above it was a fearsome black mosaic dog, promising trouble for anyone who threatened the inhabitants of this house!

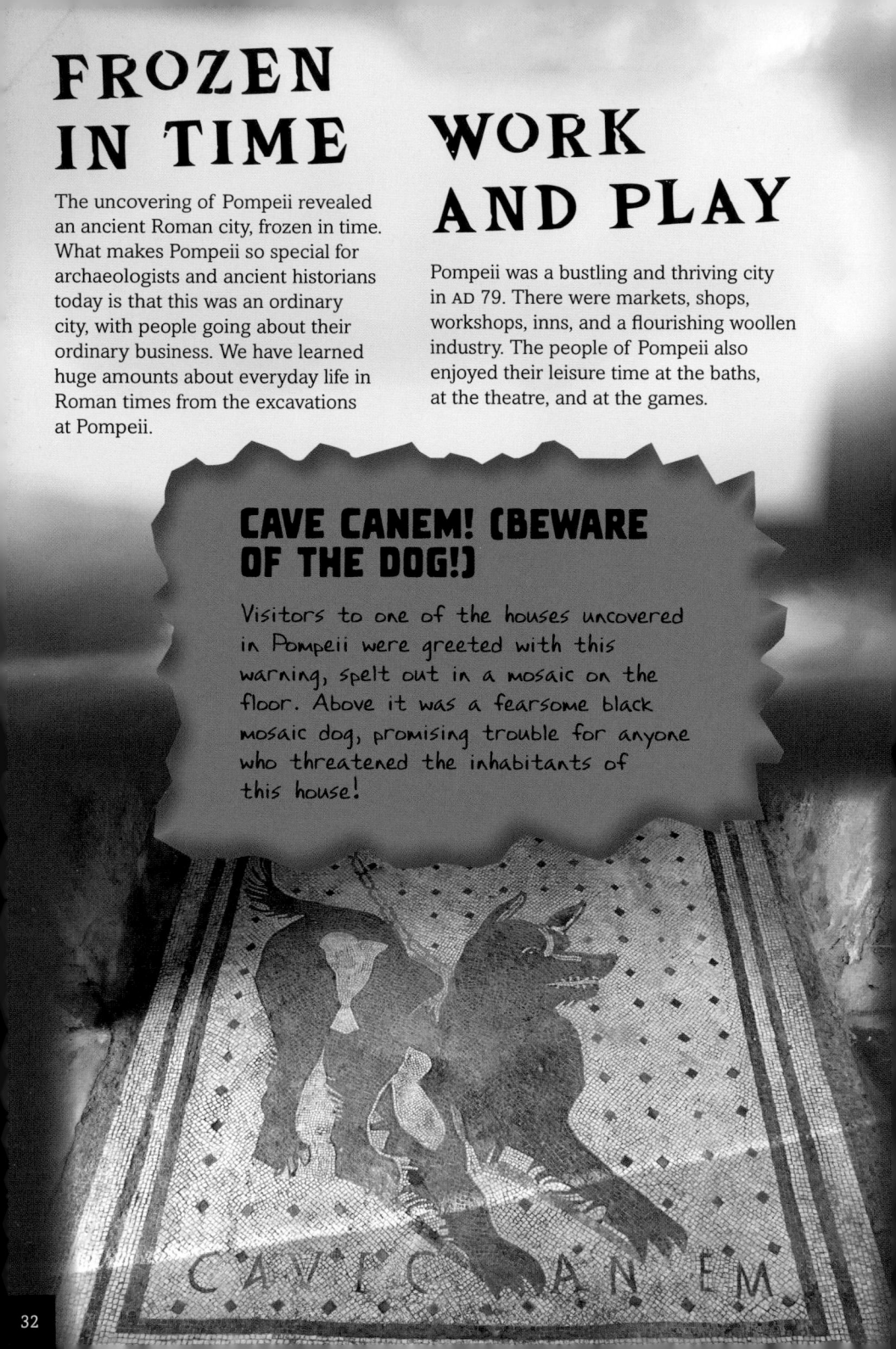

What did people eat in Pompeii? When Vesuvius erupted there was bread baking in the ovens at the city's many bakeries. In some cases, the volcanic ash from the eruption sealed the ovens, preserving the loaves of bread inside. It is extremely unusual for items of food to survive over the centuries.

The incredible heat of the eruption preserved not only the loaves of bread but also eggs, walnuts and almonds, dates, figs and olives. A popular speciality was a smelly fish sauce called garum, which the Pompeiians used a bit like tomato ketchup. It was a sauce to go with everything!

This ancient Roman bread was preserved in the bakers' ovens at Pompeii by the eruption of Vesuvius.

LOST CITIES OF THE INCAS

For nearly 100 years the Incas ruled over an expanding empire that eventually stretched 3,620 kilometres (2,249 miles) down the western coast of South America. The Inca's capital was Cuzco, a city high in the Andes Mountains.

When Spanish *conquistadors* (conquerors) began to explore Inca territory in the 1520s, it soon became clear to them that this was a wealthy land, with possibilities for great riches and treasure…

TAKING ADVANTAGE

In 1532, a small force of Spanish *conquistadors* under the command of Francisco Pizarro returned to the land of the Incas. They found the empire in turmoil. An outbreak of smallpox had killed many thousands of people, and a bitter civil war had just come to an end. The Spanish were quick to take advantage of the weak state of the empire. They captured the Inca emperor Atahualpa, and held him hostage.

THE RANSOM

As the price for his freedom, Atahualpa offered the Spanish *conquistadors* enough gold to fill the room he was imprisoned in, as well as silver to fill two more rooms. The Incas delivered the ransom – but the *conquistadors* killed Atahualpa anyway.

The Inca Empire was indeed a land of great riches. At Potosi, high in the Andes, the Spanish found a mountain that was seemingly made of silver. They established a mining town there in 1546, which quickly became one of the wealthiest towns in the world. From Potosi, thousands of tonnes of silver were transported to the coast and across the Atlantic Ocean to Spain.

INCA DEFIANCE

The Spanish *conquistadors* chose a new Inca leader, Manco Inca, to act as emperor under their direction. But Manco Inca defied the Spanish and retreated first to the wild Vitcos valley, and then to a stronghold in the remote mountainous region of Vilcabamba.

The Incas continued to mount raids against the Spanish until 1572, when the last Inca ruler was captured and executed. Vitcos and Vilcabamba were destroyed by the Spanish and left to disappear into the jungle.

LOST CITIES AND TREASURE

Ever since the fall of the Incas, there have been legends of lost Inca cities and hidden Inca treasure. Many stories tell how wealthy Incas, fleeing from the Spanish invaders, hid vast treasure troves of gold, silver, and precious stones.

Documents written by Spanish explorers in the 1500s and 1600s describe Inca cities rich in gold, silver, and gemstones. Such tales attracted many treasure hunters, explorers, and archaeologists to go looking for Inca sites in the 20th century. One of these was Hiram Bingham.

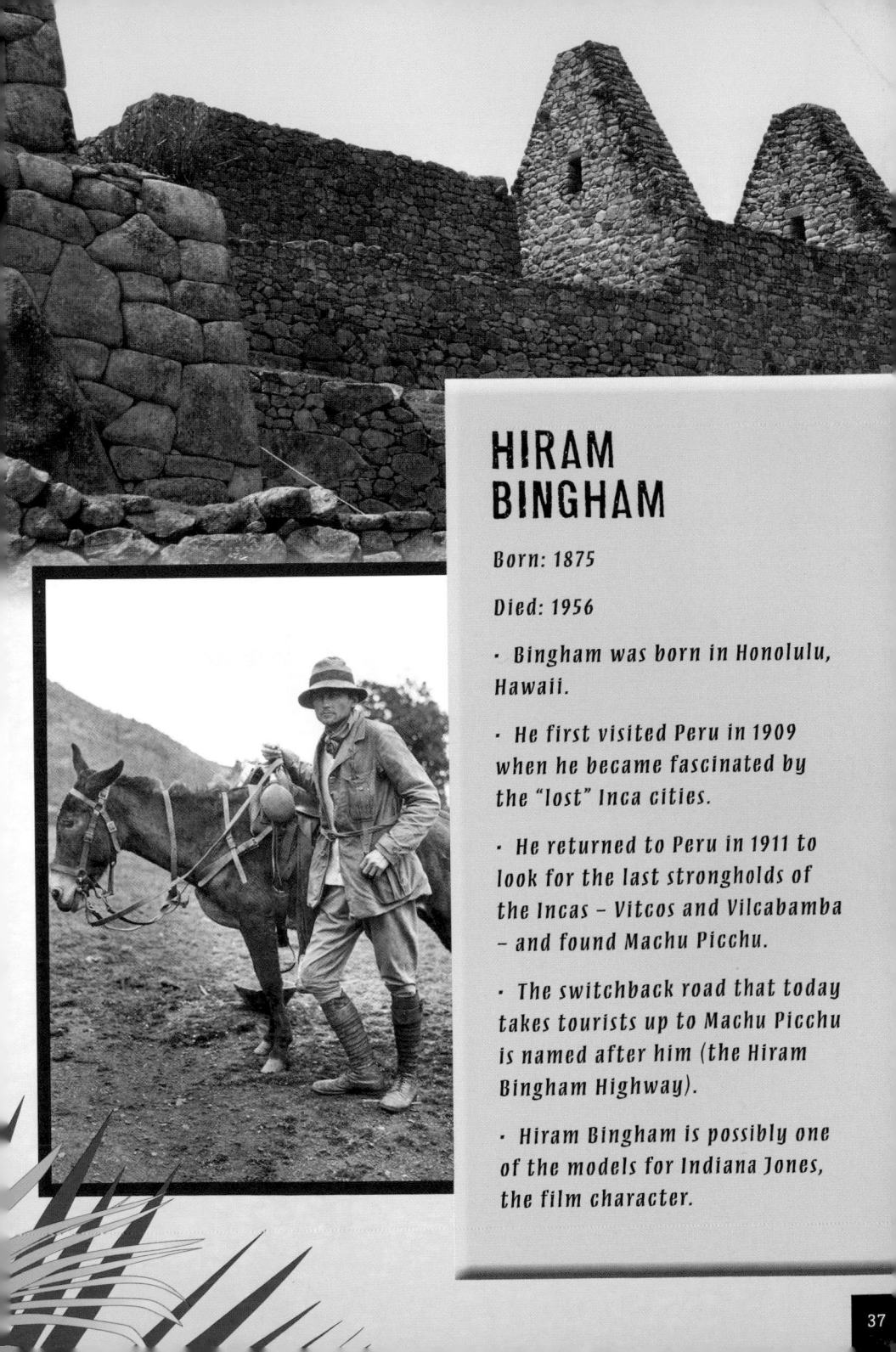

HIRAM BINGHAM

Born: 1875

Died: 1956

- Bingham was born in Honolulu, Hawaii.
- He first visited Peru in 1909 when he became fascinated by the "lost" Inca cities.
- He returned to Peru in 1911 to look for the last strongholds of the Incas – Vitcos and Vilcabamba – and found Machu Picchu.
- The switchback road that today takes tourists up to Machu Picchu is named after him (the Hiram Bingham Highway).
- Hiram Bingham is possibly one of the models for Indiana Jones, the film character.

ALONG THE TRAIL

In 1911, Hiram Bingham set off from Cuzco on a trail down the Urubamba valley to look for one of the last Inca strongholds, Vitcos. In his account of the journey, Bingham describes vividly the deep valley with the rushing rapids of the Urubamba River at the bottom, and soaring, snow-covered mountain peaks above. Sometimes he sees evidence of Inca ruins – old walls, and terraced hillsides used for growing crops. Often, the trail is little more than a narrow path cut out of the side of a sheer precipice.

MACHU PICCHU

After six days of travelling, Bingham camped near a small village. A local man offered to show him some ruins at a place called Machu Picchu. So the next day, Bingham set off after his guide. They crossed the roaring rapids of the river on a shaky rope bridge made of "four tree trunks bound together with vines". Then they climbed up through thick jungle and across steep mountain slopes. Finally, Bingham saw the ruins the guide had told him about.

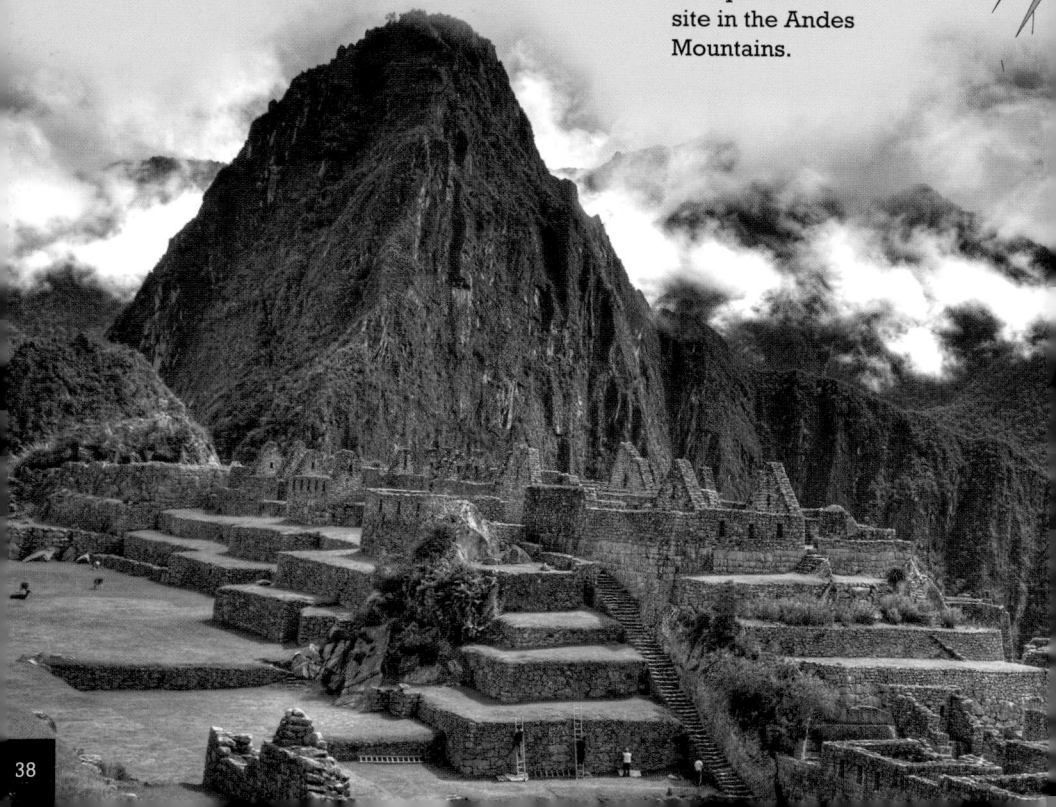

Machu Picchu is a spectacular site in the Andes Mountains.

"...WE COULD MAKE OUT A MAZE OF ANCIENT WALLS, THE RUINS OF BUILDINGS MADE OF BLOCKS OF GRANITE, SOME OF WHICH WERE BEAUTIFULLY FITTED TOGETHER IN THE MOST REFINED STYLE OF INCA ARCHITECTURE ... THE SUPERIOR CHARACTER OF THE STONE WORK ... LED ME TO BELIEVE THAT MACHU PICCHU MIGHT PROVE TO BE THE LARGEST AND MOST IMPORTANT RUIN DISCOVERED IN SOUTH AMERICA SINCE THE DAYS OF THE SPANISH CONQUEST."

HIRAM BINGHAM'S DESCRIPTION OF MACHU PICCHU IN THE NATIONAL GEOGRAPHIC MAGAZINE, 1913

WORLDWIDE FAME

The Spanish *conquistadors* never found Machu Picchu, but it was well known to local people, and it's likely that other outsiders had visited it before Bingham. Bingham returned to Peru in 1912 and 1915, and he wrote many magazine articles and books about Machu Picchu. Around the world, people were amazed and fascinated by this beautiful Inca ruin.

WHAT WAS IT?

What do we know about Machu Picchu? Most archaeologists believe that it was built as a kind of country estate for the Inca emperor Pachacuti who ruled from 1438 to 1471, the height of the Inca Empire. Others believe that it was a place for religious worship.

The Incas constructed stone walls and buildings without using mortar to hold the stones together. They cut the blocks of stone so that they all fitted snugly together. The fit is often so perfect that not even a blade of grass would slide between the stones.

NEW HOME

Bingham did not find great treasure at Machu Picchu, but he did remove more than 46,000 fragments and artefacts including pottery and stone objects. These were taken back to Yale University in the United States. In 2010, just in time for the anniversary celebration of Bingham's discovery of Machu Picchu, Yale agreed to return them. They may not be gold or silver treasure, but they are of great interest to archaeologists. Now they will have a new home in a museum in the old Inca capital, Cuzco.

LEGENDS OF LOST CITIES

Lost cities have fascinated adventurers, explorers, and treasure hunters for centuries. The work of uncovering lost cities, particularly Pompeii, led to the development of the science of archaeology. Today, new sites continue to be discovered, and each one adds to our knowledge of the past.

FACT OR FICTION?

Some lost cities may not exist. The legendary city, Atlantis, was first mentioned by the ancient Greek writer Plato, and has inspired explorers and writers ever since. Over the centuries, there have been many claims for the location of Atlantis, from the Atlantic Ocean to Antarctica. Atlantis may never be found – but then, people once thought that Troy was a mythical city!

Stories abound about the City of the Caesars on the southernmost tip of South America. It is said to have been founded by survivors of a Spanish shipwreck. Some legends say it was inhabited by huge giants, others by ghosts.

City underwater

Port Royal on the island of Jamaica was once a centre for the pirates who raided Spanish treasure ships. Then, in 1692, a massive earthquake struck. In one devastating blow, Port Royal and its inhabitants disappeared beneath the waves! In the 1980s, underwater archaeologists located the city and revealed some of its treasures. Several buildings lay on the seabed almost intact. Archaeologists found objects such as Chinese porcelain cups and bowls, pewter candlesticks, and silver forks and spoons.

LOOKING FOR LOST CITIES

Today, excavating lost cities is the work of trained archaeologists. But the thrill of finding something new remains. Have you got what it takes to search for lost cities? As well as learning about archaeology, you'll need to be fit, brave, and able to endure harsh conditions. Most of all, to make the next great discovery you'll need to be lucky!

TIMELINE

c.2500 BC
The rise of the city of Ubar in southern Arabia.

c.700s BC
The Greek poet Homer writes the *Iliad*.

AD 62
An earthquake devastates large areas of Pompeii in Italy.

AD 79 (24 August)
Mount Vesuvius erupts for the first time in 300 years, destroying the city of Pompeii in southern Italy.

c. AD 300
The collapse of the city of Ubar into the desert.

c.1250
Cahokia is one of biggest cities in the world, with a population of up to 20,000. By 1400, it is abandoned.

1438
The start of the Inca Empire in South America.

1438-1471
The possible date of construction of the city of Machu Picchu.

1532
Pizarro and his *conquistadors* invade the Inca Empire.

1533
Execution of the Inca king Atahualpa by the Spanish.

1546
The Spanish establish the mining town of Potosi in present-day Peru.

1572
The Spanish execute the last Sapa Inca (king) and destroy the Inca settlements of Vitcos and Vilcabamba.

late 1500s
The rediscovery of Pompeii by Domenico Fontana.

1763
A stone with the inscription *Rei publicae Pompeianorum* is uncovered at Pompeii.

1860
Italian archaeologist Giuseppe Fiorelli takes charge of excavations at Pompeii.

1871
Heinrich Schliemann begins excavations to uncover Troy.

1911
American explorer Hiram Bingham is led to the ruins of Machu Picchu.

1912 and 1915
Bingham returns to Peru, partly funded by Yale University.

1931
British explorer Bertram Thomas is the first European to cross the Rub al-Khali.

1945
"Priam's treasure" is taken by Soviet troops to Moscow.

1991-1992
American filmmaker Nicholas Clapp leads an expedition to find Ubar.

1993
"Priam's treasure" is put on display at the Pushkin Museum in Moscow.

2011
Yale University in the United States agrees to return artefacts from Machu Picchu to Peru.

GLOSSARY

amateur person who is interested in a subject but does not have a qualification or formal training in it

archaeologist scientist who specializes in archaeology

archaeology the study of the human past by examining remains and ruins such as burial sites and ancient cities

arrogant having an exaggerated sense of one's own importance

artefact anything made by humans, particularly something from the past

besiege to surround with hostile forces

bunker defensive fortification, usually underground

camel caravan long line of camels used to transport goods, often across desert regions

conquistadors the Spanish "conquerors" who invaded Central and South America in the 16th century

epic poem long poem that tells a story

frankincense resin, rather like gum, that comes from the trunks of Boswellia trees in southern Arabia

Gold Rush rush of people to an area where gold has been discovered. The most famous event of this type was the California Gold Rush in the 1840s, when gold was discovered in the Rocky Mountains of North America.

indigo dye natural blue dye extracted from plants

inscription words or symbols carved into a stone or other object

Islam worldwide religion that began in Arabia in the 7th century. Followers of Islam are called Muslims. Muslims believe in one God, called Allah.

mortar paste that holds bricks and stones together in a wall

mosaic picture made up of tiny pieces of stone, glass, or other materials. The Romans often decorated their houses with mosaic floors.

nomadic describes a lifestyle in which people move from place to place rather than settling in one spot

pewter metal made from a mixture of tin with a small amount of another metal, often copper or lead

porcelain type of very fine china

precipice steep and high rockface

pyroclastic flow dense mass of hot ash, lava fragments, and gases ejected explosively from a volcano, usually at great speed

Qur'an holy book of Islam

satellite object that is sent into orbit around Earth by humans

sinkhole hole in the ground formed when the roof of an underground cave collapses

smallpox highly infectious disease caused by a virus. It was unknown in the Americas before the arrival of Europeans in the 15th century.

Soviet the Soviet Union, or USSR, was the Communist state that existed between 1922 and 1991

Space Shuttle space aeroplane that flew between Earth and the orbiting International Space Station from 1981 until 2011

FIND OUT MORE

Books

Digging for Troy: From Homer to Hisarlik, Jill Rubalcaba and Eric Cline (Charlesbridge Publishing, 2011)

Pompeii (Lost Worlds and Mysterious Civilizations), Heather Lehr Wagner (Chelsea House, 2012)

The Adventures of Odysseus & The Tale of Troy: Homer's Great Epics (re-written for children), Padraic Colum (Tark Classic Fiction, 2007)

The Inca Empire (Time Travel Guides), Jane Bingham (Raintree, 2007)

Usborne Encyclopedia of the Ancient World, Jane Bingham, Fiona Chandler, Jane Chisholm (Usborne, 2007)

Volcanoes and Earthquakes (Eyewitness), Susanna van Rose (Dorling Kindersley, 2008)

Websites

www.bbc.co.uk/history/ancient/romans/pompeii_rediscovery_01.shtml
Visit this BBC website to learn more about the excavations and discoveries in the doomed city of Pompeii.

video.nationalgeographic.com/video/kids/people-places-kids/peru-machupicchu-kids
On this National Geographic website you can watch a film of Machu Picchu as it is today.

www.saudiaramcoworld.com/issue/198903/crossing.the.rub..htm
This diary account of what it's like to cross the vast Rub al-Khali desert was written by American traveller Eric Mandaville.

www.saudiaramcoworld.com/issue/198606/the.wabar.meteorite.htm
Philby's discoveries in the Rub al-Khali are explored on this site.

Places to visit

British Museum
Great Russell Street
London WC1B 3DG
www.britishmuseum.org

The British Museum has collections from all over the world, including ancient Rome and the Americas.

If you get the chance, you could also visit the site at Pompeii, Italy, and the National Archaeological Museum in Naples, which houses many of the artefacts taken from Pompeii.

Topics for Further research

- Find out more about the Cahokia earth mounds – who built them, and why (cahokiamounds.org)
- See what you can find out about the British explorer, Harry St John Philby. He had a very famous son. See if you can find out what made him famous.
- Inspired by Heinrich Schliemann, another amateur archaeologist called Arthur Evans excavated the site at Knossos in Greece. You can see much of what he found in the Ashmolean Museum in Oxford. Who lived at Knossos?
- El Dorado was a famous lost empire in South America, famed for its gold and wealth. In 1541, a *conquistador* called Gonzalo Pizarro, plunged into the jungle with a group of 300 fellow-soldiers in search of El Dorado. See what you can find out about the legend of El Dorado.

INDEX

archaeological excavations 13, 15, 19, 23, 30–31
archaeologists 7, 43
Atahualpa 34, 35, 44
Atlantis 42

Bedouin 9, 10, 11, 15
Bingham, Hiram 6, 7, 36, 37–39, 40, 41, 44

Cahokia 5, 44, 47
Calvert, Frank 18
camel caravans 11, 13, 15
Challenger Space Shuttle 11
City of the Caesars 42
Clapp, Nicholas 12
conquistadors 34–35, 36, 40, 44
Cuzco 34, 41

earthquakes 24, 43
El Dorado 47
Evans, Arthur 47

Fiennes, Ranulph 12
Fiorelli, Giuseppe 30–31
fish sauce 29, 33
food 29, 33
frankincense 8, 9, 15

glassware 28
gold and silver 21, 35, 36, 43

hidden treasure 36
Hisarlik 18, 19, 20–22, 23
Homer 17, 19, 20

Iliad 17, 18, 19, 44
Inca civilization 6, 34–41, 44

Jamaica 43
jewellery 21, 22, 28

Knossos 47

Machu Picchu 6, 7, 37, 38–41, 44
Manco Inca 36
Mohenjo-Daro 4
mosaics 30, 32
museums 47
mythical cities 42

natural disasters 5, 24–29, 43
nomadic peoples 9

Pachacuti 40
Philby, Harry St John 10–11, 12, 47
pirates 43
Pizarro, Francisco 34, 44
Pizarro, Gonzalo 47
plaster casts 30, 31
Plato 42
Pliny the Younger 25, 29
Pompeii 5, 24–33, 44
Port Royal 43
Potosi 35, 44
pottery and porcelain 15, 41, 43
Priam 20
"Priam's Treasure" 21–23

Qur'an 9

Romans 24–29, 32–33
Rub Al-Khali 8–15, 44

satellite images 12
Schliemann, Heinrich 16–23
Shis'r 12, 13, 14–15
sinkhole 14
smallpox 34
snakes 13
South America 34–41, 42, 47
stone wall construction 39, 40

Thomas, Bertram 10, 44
treasure hunters 30, 36
Trojan War 17, 20, 44
Troy 16–23, 44

Ubar 10, 11, 12, 14–15, 44

Vesuvius 5, 24–29, 44
Vilcabamba 36, 37, 44
Vitcos 36, 37, 38, 44
volcanic eruptions 5, 24–29

warfare 5, 23

Zarins, Juris 12